REFLECTIONS, REMINISCENCES,
& MEMORIES

Borgo Press Books by LORENE E. BURGESS

Reflections, Reminiscences, & Memories: Selected Poems

REFLECTIONS, REMINISCENCES, & MEMORIES

SELECTED POEMS

LORENE E. BURGESS

THE BORGO PRESS
MMXI

Borgo Laureate Series
ISSN 0182-3336

Number Eight

REFLECTIONS, REMINISCENCES, & MEMORIES

Copyright © 2011 by Lorene E. Burgess

FIRST EDITION

Published by Wildside Press LLC

www.wildsidebooks.com

DEDICATION

To the Memory of My Parents,

Nellie Elizabeth Green and Emil Burgess;

And to my **family**, who encouraged me;

And special thanks to my sister, **Emilia Burgess Linder**, who organized and typed my verses long before I had a computer to do my own work. She and her husband, **Art Linder**, assembled some of my earlier poems in booklet form;

Many thanks also to **Michael Burgess**, for suggesting this book, and editing and publishing it for me—and giving me the shove to get it moving!

CONTENTS

Introduction. 9
Reflections and Reminiscences. 11
Memories 205
The Year of the Rabbit 278
Index of Poems 280
About the Author 285

INTRODUCTION

I have been writing verses as long as I can remember, most of which are now lost in the mists of time.

I worked most of my life as a registered nurse, enjoying a long, happy career until my retirement. There were other routes I would have enjoyed pursuing, but nursing was my "calling," and I have no regrets about following it. I enjoyed all lines of nursing, but home health was my favorite and final field of practice.

One consequence of this is that I often found myself attending my patients' funerals, which eventually led to my writing eulogies for their wakes. Many of these are included in this little book of verse—and for all too many of the individuals memorialized, my words are one of the few records of their passing. They deserved more.

I have many interests, including genealogy, poetry, bird-watching, working puzzles and word games, collecting old books, art prints, seashells, rocks, and music of all kinds. I enjoy spending time with my family and friends. I also like just to sit on my porch and feed the birds.

I owe special thanks to Sister Emilia Burgess Linder,

who helped organize and type my verses long before I had a computer to do my own. She and her husband, Art Linder, assembled some of my earlier verses into booklet form.

Many thanks also to Michael Burgess, for suggesting this book, and editing and publishing it for me through his Borgo Press imprint. He gave me the necessary shove to get it moving!

If you enjoy my book, please e-mail me at:

lburgess@cmaaccess.com

—Lorene E. Burgess
Monroe, Louisiana
December 4, 2010

REFLECTIONS AND REMINISCENCES

REMEMBRANCE

Come sit beside me,
Let's talk for a spell.
Perhaps you will listen
As my story I tell.

We grew up together,
Time tore us apart;
Yet I long to tell you
The things in my heart.

How our parents loved us,
And they did their best,
While praying and trusting
To God for the rest.

They worked beside us
All the days through,
And they stood behind us
In all we did too.

The times were not easy,
Yes, times then were hard;

Their bodies grew weary,
Their hands were scarred.

Their formal schooling,
Just six or eight years;
They earned their living
With sweat, toil, and tears.

No college for them,
Or even high school;
They were not exceptions,
But more like the rule.

Their work began early,
Ere cock's crow began;
And when it was over,
Dark had come again.

No house they owned,
Little to call their own;
Even the earth they tilled
Was just on loan.

They farmed on "shares"
The wild un-tilled land;
They cleared and planted
And hoped for a "stand."

They chopped and picked cotton,
Planted and pulled corn,

Picked peas and dug potatoes
To dusk from early morn.

They mended the fences,
Chased cows, gathered eggs,
And probably wished for
Another pair of legs.

We children were praying
That it would rain,
While they were praying
For sunshine again.

We children wanted
To run and play,
While our parents knew
Debts they must repay.

Repay the landlord,
Two-thirds was his pay,
Just for the privilege
On his land to stay.

Next pay the seed man
For the use of his seeds;
Then pay the Physician
Who attended our needs.

With the remainder
They did their best;

So we were fed
And schooled and dressed.

So we were able
To rise above,
Born on their hopes,
Their dreams and love.

We went to college
Or learned a trade,
So we could do better
And they gave their aid.

They worked for their neighbors,
When their work was done,
In order to send us
Ten dollars or one.

For us they picked cotton,
Pulled corn and baled hay,
Cleaned houses and labored,
So we'd have a way,

A way to climb up,
And out of the mold
It took all their life,
For now they'd grow old.

Still they prayed daily
That we could do better;

Did we ever thank them
Or send them a letter?

Let's thank them now,
It will be too late;
When they have crossed over
Through life's other gate.

For my parents,
Emil and Nellie Burgess

September 10, 1982

JOYFUL REUNION

Run little girl,
Go meet your mother;
You never knew her
And you had no other.

Shifted and shuffled
From place to place,
Always wishing for her,
Though you knew not her face.

You were just five months old
When the lord took her away;
After seventy-five long years
You'll see her this day.

For her you've longed
Through many long years;
Go now to rejoin her
As you shed happy tears

She understands
All you've been through;

For she grew up
Without parents, too.

Tell her we love her
And your daddy, too;
Someday we'll meet them
When our work here is through.

For my mother,
Nellie Elizabeth Green Burgess
And her mother,
Lorena Elizabeth Adams Green

February 04, 1996

TO ONE WHO HAS CROSSED OVER

I no longer see you,
Yet this much I know;
You've traveled the path
On which I too must go.

For you, too, lived here
Amidst toil and strife,
Along paths that lead us
Into eternal life.

You too suffered doubts,
Troubles and fears,
Yet hoped for the best,
And sometimes shed tears.

Yet did you trust
In our Father above,
To right the wrongs,
For you knew his love.

You said you were ready
For he'd come to you,

To say he'd be with you
And help you through.

You bade me good-bye,
As your sight grew dim,
I too, felt his presence,
And knew you were with Him.

I sat close beside you
As angel choirs did sing,
As you safely crossed over
To our Savior and King.

On this final journey
You were not alone;
He came to receive you
As one of His own.

Dedicated to the memory of my Father,
Emil Burgess, who died May 3, 1972

November 11, 1972

MOTHER

In all the Earth
There is no other
Who cares for you
Like your dear own mother.

She loved you always
From the very start,
As she carried you in
And under her heart.

A part of her
You'll always be,
Now and forever
Through all eternity.

For *Nellie Elizabeth Green Burgess*
September 12, 1919 to September 17, 1994

May 9, 2004

PRECIOUS MEMORIES

Deep in my heart
And in my soul
Linger precious memories
Of Christmases of old.

Money was scarce,
And conveniences, too;
No matter times were poor,
Our parents always came through.

No money for gifts,
Their resources were few,
They made many things,
So we'd have something new.

Pea shooters and rag dolls,
To name just a few,
Scarves, purses, and undies,
And paper dolls, too.

Daddy always found a tree
Out in the back,
So for decoration
We would not lack.

We made popcorn balls,
And strung some for the tree;
We made chains, stars and angels,
Our decorations were free.

On Christmas morning
We'd rush to see,
What Santa had left
Us under the tree.

A shoebox would be left
On our own chair,
Overflowing with goodies,
Enough to share.

Oranges and apples,
Nuts and candy, too;
A coin would be hidden
In our apples or our shoe.

We had so much,
And our needs were few;
How much I wish
You'd known those times, too.

Thanks to our parents,
Nellie and Emil Burgess,
for our precious memories

December 24, 2005

A LEGEND IN HIS OWN TIME

I first heard of
Jim Thompson today,
When you told me
He had "passed away."

Jim lived in a house
Beside the road,
Where anyone could stop
And rest and "unload."

And everybody who was,
Anybody at all,
Sooner or later dropped in
On Jim to "call."

He treated each visit
As an occasion,
For his friends of every
Race and persuasion.

Nourishment he provided
For the body and soul;

A teller of tales,
A storyteller, I'm told.

He knew everyone's history,
Both black and white;
And I hear he wasn't
Afraid of a fight.

His friends came from far,
And they came from near,
All the old legends
And stories to hear.

Like some forgotten ancestor
From the beginning of man,
Reciting lineage and stories,
Village elder, historian.

June 24, 1996

DREAM OF ANOTHER

You dream of another
Time and place
That lives on in
Memory's fond embrace.

Did you ever dive
From Glorieta Mirador
At full tide on
That Pacific Shore?

Or wear the scarlet cape
Of the Picador,
Receive honor and homage
As a brave matador?

Did you sing or play
With a Mariachi Band
In that distant
Beloved fabled land?

Or throw the net
Out far and wide
To reap the bounty

Of the great gulf tide?

Or from Cabo San Lucas'
Outermost reaches,
Or from the tranquil
Sea of Cortes beaches?

Does the Civil War
Still forever rage,
As it did in
Every forgotten age?

Is there still
Lack of respect
For the descendents
Of the noble Aztec?

Does the color
Of your skin
Divide you now
As it did then?

In that long-ago battle,
The war of 1821,
Independence from Spain
Was finally won.

But the Indian still fights
The Spaniard's son,
All across from Tampico
To old Mazatlán.

Did you cross the big river,
The Rio Grande,
Seeking a new life
In this "Promised Land?"

How do you fare
In this alien place,
Alongside men
Born of every race?

In this great land
Of "Milk and Honey,"
So many men
Seek fame and money.

You must not forget
Mexico's grand lore,
Passed down to you
From days of yore.

Its beginnings remain
Shrouded in mystery,
Your heritage lies
In its ancient history,

Dedicated to the employees of
Chile Verde of Monroe, Louisiana

November 3, 1996

AUTUMN GLORY

The earth is ablaze
With bright Autumnal hue,
Flaming reds and gold
Under skies of gray-blue.

A mantle of rich color,
From leaves drifting down,
Forms red-golden carpets
To blanket the ground.

A whisper, a rustle,
Bright leaves all around,
In a riot of color:
Scarlet and golden brown.

Flaming orange, burnished copper,
And bright golden yellow;
Each tree's in its glory
Trying to outshine its fellow.

October 31, 1982

THE REGAL PINE

In lofty branches
Of the soaring pine,
Mournful sighing winds
Whimper and whine.

In courtly dance
Before the winds,
Leaning and bowing,
Its trunk bends.

Dipping and swaying
In the breeze
Are tender branches
Of soft-wooded trees.

Before the elements
It bends and gives,
In graceful submission,
And so it lives.

It stands so tall,
Its branches sing,

It is the wise
Proud forest king.

October 1, 1995

THESE I HAVE SEEN

I have seen
Ocean spray,
Conch shells floating
In the Bay.

Graceful silver fish
In joyous flight,
Over golden waters
Kissed by moonlight.

I have seen
Great waves unfold,
In eternal waters
Of molten gold.

Lighted freighters,
Ships at sea,
Neptune's depths
Flowing endlessly.

February 3, 1996

OMEN

Torrents cascade,
Crashing down,
Lightning bolts flashing,
Earthward bound.

Thunder rumbling
With awesome sound;
Ominous portent,
Malevolence profound.

Depraved winds shrieking
With mournful sound,
Then frenzied elements
Quiet down.

Rain clouds black
As any tunnel
Rush merging together
To form a funnel.

Heavy silence oppressive,
Stillness without form,

Quietly sits and waits
In the eye of the storm.

August 20, 1995

CAMOUFLAGE

Fog thick and heavy,
Moving without sound,
Wet mists embracing,
All low to the ground.

Completely changing
Familiar scenes,
Camouflaging the earth
By devious means.

Filtering street lights
To a dull yellow gleam;
A feeling of abandonment
To some late night dream.

In curtain-hung valleys,
Hovering near streams,
Calling to mind
Rain forest scenes.

Covering, then shifting,
Silently moving on;

Giving place to sunlight
In the early gray dawn.

October 30, 1982

I WANT TO GO HOME

I want to go home,
Back to yesteryear,
To be once again,
With loved ones so dear.

I want to go back
To all the old places,
With loved ones to share,
And see all their faces.

I want to go home,
Where times were good,
Where everyone did
All the things they should.

No locks on the doors,
No windows nailed tight,
You could lie down in peace,
And rest well at night.

If we could go back
For an hour or a day,

Just think of the things
We'd all like to say.

In memory of my rural upbringing in Richland Parish, Louisiana, in a simpler time.

2002

ADAMS REUNION

Each year at this time
We like to meet
All our dear loved ones,
And new ones to greet.

You special folks
Are my mother's kin,
I wish you had known her
As she was back then.

She loved everyone
And called all men brother;
We were so proud
She was our mother.

She was an honor
To the Adams' name;
She always helped others
And never sought fame.

Her own dear mother
Neither she nor we knew;

Lorena Adams died
When she was only twenty-two.

In the Oklahoma Plains,
Where the wind always blows,
Our spirits seek hers—
I wonder if she knows?

For my mother,
Nellie Elizabeth Green Burgess,
and her mother,
Lorena Elizabeth Adams Green,
who died when Mama was only 5 months old.

May 19, 2005

LEGENDARY JUNIOR COLLINS

When he rode the rails,
With a whistle and a whine,
Everyone knew Junior Collins
Was on the Long Fork line.

He made that thing whimper
And whistle and bawl;
He made that great train
Give a high lonesome squawl.

He was a legend
They'll never forget;
Somewhere in that holler
The sound echoes yet.

Folks still remember
As they sit and sigh,
And swear they still hear
Junior Collins pass by.

For my grandfather,
Louis Hampton Green, Brakeman,

born in Kentucky,
and for all the men of the rails.

May 5, 2007

AUTUMN

Autumn retreats
In a blaze of glory;
Wondrous sight,
This annual story.

August 31, 1983

FOG

Primeval mist,
Vapor-shrouded,
Diffuse pale halos
Round lampposts crowded.

Invading open spaces
Under bare-branched trees;
Cool misty veiling
Of rooftop eaves.

Pervasive grayness
Whispering in;
Softly stealing
Out again.

March 6, 1984

WHAT THEN?

When rivers run
Red with blood,
When water taps
Give only mud.

When earth no longer
Has arable soil,
You'll starve no matter
How hard you toil.

When mountains fall
In a great landslide,
And you vainly search
For a place to hide.

When the moon is dark
And great oceans rise,
And the sun no longer
Lights up the skies.

When two hundred million
Cross the plain,

Another third of mankind
Will be brutally slain.

As mankind continues
On its path of sin,
What, oh what,
Will you do then?

What, oh what,
Oh sinful men,
What, oh what,
Will you do then?

November 9, 1995

MISSING YOU

Here of late
Oft times it seems
The child of my youth
Exists only in dreams.

Gone forever
The younger me,
Though remnants remain,
They are hard to see.

Where are you now?
Where did you go?
I am still me,
But I miss you so.

I fulfilled many dreams
For you and me,
Perhaps in this life,
I didn't fail thee.

Child of my youth
Stay close to me;

Always together,
Forever we'll be.

March 6, 2007

DREAM VISITS

In dreams I can see
Ancestors from afar,
Speaking their language
Around their tipi fire.

And when I awake
To find them gone,
I still remember
Their ancient song.

So happy am I
To be blessed, it seems,
To meet my ancestors
Late night in my dreams.

To unknown ancestors who traverse my dreams

May 17, 2006

CLOUD ON THE GROUND

Refreshing cool mist,
Vapor all around;
Early morning pleasure,
Cloud on the ground.

December 4, 2002

WHEREVER FLOWERS GROW

Each time I see
The dew on the rose,
I'll always remember
You gave me those.

You left a memory
So sweet and true,
Wherever flowers grow,
I'll think of you.

Eulogy for the wake of *Elizabeth Sledge*.
Her roses still bloom in my yard.

September 22, 1997

LEGACY

A flawed time,
Innocence scarred,
Not a trusting time,
Mankind has grown hard.

Razors and needles
Are no Halloween treat;
Now they are putting arsenic
Into the food we eat.

Hatred lust and envy
These days pervade;
Rape, murder, and insanity
Characterize this decade.

What evil possesses us
To stir up such strife?
Nothing now is sacred,
Not even life.

Dear God who created
The free-willed man,

We've had as much free will
As we think we can stand.

Dear Lord and Creator,
To us draw near;
Our hearts are heavy,
And we faint with fear.

October 10, 1982

WINTER RAIN

No sky-splitting torrent
Nor wind-tossed deluge,
A quiet steady fall
Of rain drops so huge.

Drops clinging to fences
And hugging the ground,
Evenly covering the earth
With dampness all around.

Steady and solemn,
Not frolicsome you,
Blanketing the grass,
Silent as dew.

October 30, 1982

SHE SITS AND WAITS

She sits and waits
In her lonely room,
As cold and dark
As any tomb.

"They said the world
Was coming to an end,"
She tells the nurse,
Her only friend.

Her "kids" are gone,
Her money they spent;
She has no idea
Where either went.

Gas was turned off,
Electricity too;
What's a poor soul
Like she to do?

March 9, 1996

SEASONS

What's happened to Autumn?
She passed through one day,
Wearing beauty like a garland,
But she didn't stop to play.

Summer's still here,
As though reluctant to go,
And leave us to deal with
Winter's cold ice and snow.

Winter has made plans
To stop by any day,
For a very long visit
She's planned to stay.

We so enjoyed summer
And Autumn we'll miss,
As we prepare for
Dread Winter's cool kiss.

Oh how we long for
The freshness of Spring:

Daffodils and robins,
And jonquils she'll bring.

October 7, 1982

AN UNGRATEFUL LOT

Surely we are
An ungrateful lot,
Never contented
With what we've got.

The water is too hot,
Or else too cold;
We are too young,
Or else we're too old.

The weather is either
Too cold or too hot;
Always we're wishing
For something that's not.

We are too fat,
Or else we're too thin;
Lord, why not just junk us
And start over again?

Do you ever regret
Having made man,

To be the star
Of your creation plan?

December 6, 1977

TO THOSE WHO MURDER

You hurt and you murder,
And kill the bright dreams,
So full of ill will,
You harbor hatred, it seems.

Why can't you respect
And love one another?
Who gave you the right
To destroy your brother?

You rob and you kill
With a gun or a knife.
How dare you to take
Another man's life?

Who gave you the right,
Permission, if you will,
To rape and to plunder,
To maim and to kill?

Did you make man?
Is he yours to destroy?

He's a priceless creation,
Not some trifling toy.

And what of yourself?
You must answer to
The God who made him,
And also made you.

You were created
With a free will,
And with it you chose
On this day to kill.

In choosing to go
Your own willful way,
You sealed your own doom
On this fateful day.

In memory of the brutal murders of two ladies who did not deserve such a horrible end—one a neighbor, the other a well-beloved minister.

October 22, 1982

HOME AT LAST

Home at last!
To your place of birth
Your mortal remains
Will return to earth.

Rejoin your parents
And your second-born,
As we bear witness
This sad fateful morn.

Your faithful husband
Has brought you here,
From a great distance
To those you held dear.

Troubles are over,
All pain is past,
All sorrow is ended,
You are home at last.

For the graveside services of my dear cousin,
Kathy (Gettis Kathleen Green) Sargeant
Alto, Louisiana

February 20, 1996

IT'S THE LIVING
I'LL MISS

I don't dread the dying:
It's the living I'll miss,
So don't you be crying,
Come give me a kiss.

I'll keep getting ready,
For soon I must leave;
Just keep strong and steady,
And try not to grieve.

The one who is leaving
Is the one who is sad;
Regretting to leave all
The good times we've had

Someday we will meet
On heaven's bright shore;
To live there and love there
And part never more.

October 13, 1982

YOUR FAITHFUL FRIEND

Your faithful friend,
You did unload;
He sits and waits
Beside the road.

He looks each driver
In the eye,
In every car
That passes by.

Cold and hungry,
Your forsaken pet,
For your return,
Waits patiently yet.

To your memory
He is true;
He will starve
Awaiting you.

March 9, 1996

THIS TOO WILL PASS

I want to go home,
I'm ready, said he,
To sit in my own chair
Under my own shade tree.

This journey has been,
With a heavy load,
Taking me down
A long, unpaved road,

I want to go home;
I am getting tired;
I'm ready to rest
In my own back yard.

My flowers need tending,
My birds are in need,
They await fresh water,
And their special bird seed

Where are my squirrels?
Did they go away?

Or are they just over the fence
Watching for me today?

Forty-two treatments
They said I would need;
I do as they say,
Their advice I heed.

This too will pass,
As all things do;
Soon I can come home,
And start my life anew.

For my brother-in-law,
Art Linder

June 3, 2006

A NURSE'S LAMENT

This day I saw
Two men in their prime;
Little did they know
It had come their time.

One man was working
Up under his car;
In just a few seconds
He had crossed the bar.

No time to cry out,
No time to pray;
Too late forever,
He was on his way.

Where did he go?
I cannot say.
Too late to cry out,
Too late to pray.

The other was busy
Painting a wall;

He was suddenly dizzy,
Then had a great fall.

He too was dead,
As with a snap of a finger;
No time for dread,
No time to linger.

Both lives snuffed out
Without any warning,
Leaving loved ones in doubt,
Shocked, trembling, and mourning.

Were they prepared
To go to God?
Or were they snared
Too soon under the sod?

Nothing could I do
Except to pray;
Their souls would be
With God this day.

Again this day
My soul did cry,
Against needless loss
An unborn babe to die.

His mother, a girl of twenty-three,
Does not want him, you see.

He will die,
His body torn,
He will die before he's born.

He has no choice,
He's in the womb;
We'll never hear his voice,
He'll have no tomb.

His mother will receive
Only the very best;
She'll not hurt or grieve,
She'll be treated as a guest.

She'll have medicine
To relieve her pain,
While she commits
This awful sin.

She'll have ease
Upon her bed,
While her baby's body
Runs pure red.

He'll be pulled apart,
Brains, bones, and tissue,
By powerful suction,
This unwanted issue.

Torn up out of his cozy nest
Into a jar—be sure it's all there.

Shall I tell you of the rest?
Or does anyone anywhere really care?

Mother is resting well
Under heavy sedation,
No discomfort or pain
For her inconvenient duration.

This day I am weary,
Beaten, and worn;
So worn down by death
And unheeding scorn.

Lord, you did not
Intend it this way;
Please show us and guide us,
And lead us this day.

Natchez, Mississippi

December 5, 1977

THE LAMB

Look and behold,
The gentle lamb,
A symbol of
The great "I Am."

A sacrifice
He chose to be,
To pay for our sins,
And set us free.

February 3, 1996

THE DOVE

The cooing of
The gentle dove
Reminds us of
Our Father's love.

Symbol of His
Holy Spirit divine,
Given to lead
And to guide mankind.

February 3, 1996

GUARDIAN ANGEL

Guardian angel
At my side,
Keep me safe
Whate'er betide.

Lift me up,
Keep me warm,
Keep me safe
From all harm.

You were sent from God above
To represent His endless love.

January 29, 1996

EAGLE FLIGHT

Majestic eagle,
Bird of prey,
Soars high above
Earth's stone and clay.

Above the clouds
So high it flies,
Undisputed monarch
Of endless skies.

January 29, 1996

I'VE HEARD IT SAID

I've heard it said,
And believe it true,
Folks you don't like
Also don't like you.

I've always found
It to be true
That folks you do like
Will also like you.

It's all just a part
Of our Father's plan,
That we should be happy
And love our fellow man.

He gave the example
Of how we should live;
We'll always get back
If we're willing to give.

October 7, 1982

SUNSET-MOONRISE

You said a sunset big
As an old red barn.
Is that the truth?
Or is it a yarn?

I know the answer;
For the answer lies
There in the heavens,
And here in your eyes.

As the sun goes down,
The moon starts to rise;
So we'll always have
A light in the skies.

The sun is to warm us
And give us day light;
The moon is to brighten
The starry skies at night.

Both precious gifts
From our Father above;

To all here on earth
From His great love.

October 4, 1982

WINTER'S SCULPTURES

Winter's sculptures:
Ice-laden limbs
Sun-kissed to
Golden glittery trims;

Rainbow hues captured
In diamond-iced scenes;
Myriad gem sparkles
In landscapes swept clean.

December 6, 1982

AUTUMN CLOUDS

Gray clouds drifting,
Sailing by,
Swiftly passing
Through the sky.

Not stopping here,
Just passing through,
Quickly reaching places
They are headed to.

They journey onward,
How swiftly they fly;
To many miles north,
There to darken the sky.

I marked the swift passage
Of dark clouds overhead,
And knew they were headed
To other places instead.

October 9, 1982

REFLECTIONS ON ALL-HALLOWS EVE

Full moon presiding,
A crisp cool night,
Windows all ablaze
With jack-o'-lantern light.

Children are walking
All through the town,
Seeking fun and treasures;
We'll not let them down.

Front porch lights on
In a show of welcome,
Saying "you'll be safe here,"
"Try us, we're home."

We will not trick you,
But will give you a treat,
Admire your costume,
Give you popcorn to eat.

We'll pretend we're afraid
Of your bold ugly face,

Give you copper coins and candy,
Your fears to erase.

Childhood runs so swiftly,
The time is so brief;
This should be a happy time
For you, is our belief.

So much of your childhood's
Been stolen from you;
Laughter and innocence,
And "growing up" time too.

You're exposed daily
To all that is mean,
Debased human living
Fills your TV screen.

You are not allowed wonder
And growing-up space;
Youth times of yesteryear
Are now out of place.

You've missed so much
Of the great simple life;
You are exposed daily
To the world's sin and strife.

So just for tonight
Let's recapture again

Simple pleasures of life,
If only we can.

October 31, 1982

CHOOSE LIFE

With everything to gain
And nothing to lose,
It's left up to you
This day to choose.

His hand is stretched out
In forgiveness to you;
He's waiting to help
In all that you do.

He's tenderly waited
Through many long years,
To ease all your burdens
And calm all your fears.

Angel choirs are hushed,
In silence they wait;
They see you are standing,
Your hand to the gate.

They wait as you knock,
With your face to the door,

Seeking one who can give you
Peace and life evermore.

All heaven will rejoice,
Oh how they will sing,
To welcome the latest
New child of the King.

October 30, 1980

FEAR NOT

Soon we will cross over
To life's other side;
God bids us fear not
Whatever betide.

He'll walk before us
Each step of the way,
To lead and to guide us
Into that perfect day.

He has prepared for us
A place with Him,
So we need not fear
When our light grows dim.

We'll lie down to rest
And wake over there,
Where we'll live forever
In His love and care.

So come, let's get ready
To lay down our load;

Our steps will be lighter
To the end of the road.

August 23, 1982

MASTER POTTER

Who am I
To make a plan?
I can make nothing;
You made man.

You formed him from
Dust of the earth,
Into him breathed life
And gave him birth.

Designed and created
From the lowly sod,
In your own image
To be a friend of God.

August 5, 1995

TRUST HIM

The dear holy spirit
Does so tenderly woo;
He'll lead you to Jesus,
For He loves you too.

The Spirit of God
Does so strive with man,
To remind us of Jesus,
And help us understand.

That Christ is the gate
The way into life,
To help ease our sorrow
And trouble and strife.

He'll walk beside you
Each and every day;
Just learn to trust Him,
He'll show you the way.

October 30, 1982

THE HEAVENS

The Big Dipper's path
I want to trace,
When I must leave
This time and place.

I want to view
The evening star,
Virgo and Pisces,
And galaxies far.

The Andromeda Nebula
I long to see,
And Mars and Jupiter
Are waiting for me.

So don't bother to look
For me this day;
I've gone dancing
On the Milky Way.

February 10, 1997

FREEDOM

In this great nation,
So blessed are we,
So fortunate to live
In the land of the free.

We have clothes to wear
And food we have plenty,
While so many others
Scarcely have any.

We can go where we want,
We can do as we please;
Compared to many others,
We live a life of ease.

We have a roof over our heads
And shoes on our feet;
Protected we are
From the cold and the heat.

So much has been given
To you and to me;

We work hard for it,
It is not free.

Our precious children
Amidst the world's strife,
In order to save us
Often pay with their life.

Freedom we have,
But it is not free,
Bought at a great cost,
Indebted forever we'll be.

God Bless America

July 4, 2006

NOW

What say you now,
Now she is gone,
The fragile old mother
You always leaned on?

What now will you do,
Now she is gone?
She'll be here no more
For you to lean on.

You took all her money,
You took all her love,
You fight over what's left,
Does she watch from above?

She gave all she had,
There was nothing left to give;
I don't understand
How with yourself you can live.

May 5, 2007

THE LITTLE OUTHOUSE OUT BACK

We grew up
With a little outhouse;
Always there was a spider
Or a snake or a mouse.

This was our only
Place to rest,
To get out of work,
We felt we were blessed.

We had the Sears-Roebuck Catalog
To cover the walls,
And have something to read
During nature's calls.

We'd sit there so long,
We'd get stuck in the hole;
And the half of this story
Has never been told!

When we'd look back,
On our way through the slough,

You'd see a "blue runner"
Gaining on you!!

And every time
A tornado came through,
Daddy would have to get boards
And build one anew.

You truly could call it
An "outhouse";
The wind would carry it off
To somewhere about.

So some lucky neighbor
Would now have two;
Lord, what a nightmare,
But so much fun too!

November 8, 2004

SCRIBBLINGS

I scribble little
Bits of verse
On scraps of paper
From my purse.

September 14, 1982

MILLIE THE SPITZ

My white dog Millie the Spitz,
Each summer suffers from fits,
Dodging the bees,
And scratching at fleas,
Each winter Millie just sits.

July 28, 1983

JIM

I once knew a fellow named Jim,
Who climbed far out on a limb;
Jim couldn't get back,
And food he did lack,
He's now referred to as Slim!

July 23, 1983

INTENSIVE CARE

My workplace Intensive Care,
Has scenes that would curl your hair;
We try to be thrifty,
But forty out of fifty
Insist it is Expensive Care.

July 23, 1983

BOO

There was an old dog named "Boo,"
Who fell into the outdoor Loo;
Old Boo, he fell down,
Without a sound,
He's now referred to as "Boo Who."

July 23, 1983

FASHION

The clothes in my closet
I haven't worn for awhile;
I'm so glad I kept them,
They're now back in style.

But when I try them on,
I'm taken down a peg;
The size six I wore,
Will now fit my leg!

May 19, 2002

MY PRAYER

Lord, don't let me falter
When it's courage I need;
Please give me the strength
To do the right deed.

Don't let me be weak
When I should be strong;
Don't let me be meek
And be in the wrong.

Silence is not always virtue,
And can cowardly be;
Sometimes it's not easy
To be all I should be.

August 5, 1995

WHO AM I?

My heart yearns
Over precious youth,
Amidst life's turns,
Seeking truth.

"Who am I?"
You want to know;
The answer's your quest
As you onward go.

"Who made me?"
And "Why?"
"Who can tell me?"
Is your cry.

"Who out there
Will draw near,
And listen to me
And really hear?"

"Why me?" "Why now?"
"Who'll dare to care?

Reach me, teach me, love me
Is your anguished prayer.

January 6, 1984

WHY?

Sometimes in this life
What we think is the end
Of life's unpaved road
Is only a bend.

As we move forward,
Someday we will know
The reason why
We had to hurt so.

In order to gain
Only God's best,
Sometimes we must forfeit
That which is less.

Someday you will know
All the reasons why
At this particular time
You had to cry.

Keep trusting in God,
In the way He has led;

Though hard to see now,
The best lies ahead.

December 30, 2006

BURGESS REUNION 2010

There are so many of us—
I wish you knew
All of us descended
From the two of you.

Your children were seven:
Oscar, Grady, Maude Neal,
Grover, then Dewey,
Lastly Emil and Cecil.

You buried two children,
Your precious Maude Neal,
Then Dewey, your beloved son;
There's not greater pain to feel.

Oscar and Ollie
Eleven little ones bore;
Grady and Eulala had three;
Grover and Lucy had three more.

Emil and Nellie had five,
Cecil and Inez had four;

Dewey and Maude Neal's lineage
Went forth no more.

From your beloved children
Many more came,
Few have found fortune,
And even fewer fame.

You bore great sorrow,
Your children great strife,
And so it continued
To those you gave life.

Bearing your names with pride
In all that we do,
Just feel you must know
How much we love you.

Someday we will meet you,
I know you await,
To run to meet us
As we near the gate.

Then at last you will know
The children are all in,
And never more worry
When you see us again.

For *Roena Elizabeth Shirley and John Guy Burgess.*

June 13, 2010

FATHERS

Our heavenly Father
Had you in his plan
From the very beginning,
When he made man.

He knew you'd be awed,
And greatly humbled too,
When your firstborn came
To dwell here with you.

He knew you'd be ready
With each new birth,
To protect and guide
Your young on this earth.

All you have given
Reflects the great love,
Passed on to us
From the father above.

So much love we feel,
We never can say,

As we remember you
On this Father's Day.

June 20, 2010

IN THE BEGINNING

In the beginning,
From the very start,
You were living there
In your mother's heart.

So long she waited
And watched for you,
And when you came,
All her dreams came true.

You were flesh of her flesh,
And bone of her bone;
As long as she lives,
You are never alone.

And if she must go
When her life is through,
Again she'll be waiting
And watching for you.

For my mother and all my sisters and nieces,
And for Natalie and Justin on this event of the birth
of *Layton Adam Carr, May 8, 2010*

OUR FAMILY

Gradually learning
Slowly in stages,
Who our people were
Down through the ages.

Can you imagine my surprise
When I came to see
Greece, Morocco, Portugal, and Turkey
Matches in my mother's DNA family tree?

These were the highest,
Though there were others:
Belarus, Lithuania, Russia, Romania,
Close matches to my mothers.

Not too much Irish,
But Israel, Germany, France, Italy;
Wonderful surprises
In mama's ancestral tree.

Perhaps this explains
Feelings of affinity

To many cultures
And people I see.

Though I've never been there,
Kentucky and Oklahoma call to me,
As do the high steppes,
And the Mediterranean Sea.

Sometimes I visit there,
If only in my dreams;
I am at home in the world,
Or so to me it seems.

May 12, 2010

COMING TOGETHER

How wonderful it is
The kinship we feel
To our Adams, Byrds,
Woodells, and Neals.

How wonderful when
Our families meet here;
So many have come
From far and from near.

I wish our ancestors
Could know and see
So many descendants
From their family tree.

I believe they'd be happy
And honored to know,
They are remembered
By us still here below.

I believe we will see them,
I think they await,

I believe they will greet us,
As we enter heaven's gates.

For then we will know,
As we are known,
Into that blessed day
We'll go not alone.

What a wonderful gathering
That homecoming will be,
When our departed loved ones
Once more we will see.

Adams Reunion

May 15, 2010

DADDY

Did you think I didn't know?
Did you think I didn't see?—
All the things you did
That you did just for me.

Don't think I didn't know,
Don't think I didn't see,
Though I failed to thank you
For all you did for me.

So long and hard you struggled,
Your pathway to find;
You gave up your dreams
To help me follow mine.

For my father, *Emil Burgess*.

June 21, 2009

BELOVED MOTHER

A precious mother
Has left and gone on,
Knowing her children
Will soon follow along.

For them she waits
And watches each day,
Still praying they each
Can yet find their way.

She stands in the door
Crying, "Supper is ready,
Now hurry along,
I'm here with your daddy."

She rose and got dressed
In her new clothes today,
In her beautiful new body
She then flew away.

You are glad she is free
Of all struggle and strife,

But you will miss her
All the days of your life.

For *Sarah Virginia Stewart*

Oct. 2, 1914- Nov. 22, 2009

DAY OF THANKSGIVING

Corn ripe in the field,
Warm sun and cool breeze,
Vegetables to harvest,
Precious fruit on the trees.

A big golden sun,
The beautiful harvest moon,
The vast starry sky,
The call of the loon.

We still have food,
A roof overhead,
Clothes on our backs,
A warm comfortable bed.

We can still assemble
Together in this place;
We are richly blessed
Among Adam's race.

Yes, we can still meet,
And we can still pray,

For this we give thanks
On this Thanksgiving Day.

November 26, 2009

MEMORIAL DAY REMEMBRANCE

When you view the photos,
And search each brave face,
You'll see our heroes
Are born of every race.

Those who go out
To stand, guard, and fight,
Are many shades of red,
Yellow, brown, black, and white.

The American soldier
You can plainly see
Certainly didn't all come
From the same family tree.

Each one watches over
All of the others,
When they are together
As though sisters and brothers.

We must stand behind them,
We must stand as one,

Against the tide of evil
Until the battle is won.

May 25, 2009

MAMA

Mama, so often
I heard you pray,
Always out loud
Near end of day.

As I saw you there
On bended knee,
Always I knew
You were praying for me.

I still can see
Your many tears,
Your heartfelt prayers
Down through the years.

Though you've gone on
Your face I still see,
Dear precious mother,
Do you still pray for me?

For Mama:
Nellie Elizabeth Green Burgess.
May 10, 2009

HEART ATTACK AT THIRTY-FIVE

You, young man
Of thirty-five,
You're very lucky
Just to be alive.

Somehow it seems
You've neglected your health,
Forgetting it is
Your greatest wealth.

Both ends and the middle,
You burned your candle,
Always took on
More than you could handle.

Running and racing
Against the tide
Can very soon
Wear out your hide!

If you would reach
Four score and ten,

Somehow your ways
You'll have to mend.

I know the kind
Of prayers you pray:
"Lord, give me patience—
Please, right away!"

It's not so easy
To go with the flow
To a real "go-getter"
Who'll get up and go!

One whose nerves
Are strung out taut,
Doesn't always do
What that one ought.

The sad thing is
That in the ICU,
One isn't allowed
To smoke, dip, or chew.

There your privileges
Are all taken away
As we promise to discuss it—
Some other day!

So here's to you
Some good advice

We'll soon let you out—
If you act real nice!

True story, J.D. Memorial Hospital,
Natchez, Mississippi,
Circa 1978

LOOK AROUND YOU

Look around you now,
What do you see?
Everyone has problems
Same as you and me.

So long as we live
In our earthly abode,
We can be sure
We'll have our own load.

Everyone has doubts,
Everyone has fears,
Many carry burdens
Down through the years.

But I have learned
Now in my decline,
I'll never trade
Your troubles for mine!

November 7, 2010

HOME HEALTH NURSE

Into the homes
We go to share
Our knowledge with others,
And give nursing care.

Patients benefit greatly
From this new trend,
Sometimes the nurse
Is their only friend.

So much they need,
Their wants are few,
Just food and housing,
And medical care too!

They'll always greet you
With a big smile,
So glad you came to help,
And perhaps visit awhile.

So many needs
There you will find,

So many ills and woes
Afflict all mankind.

You've chosen this work
(Or it's chosen you);
So give it your best—
It's the least you can do!

November 20, 1996

TO ONE GROWN WEARY

It hurts to see you
There in your chair,
So tired and weary,
And so full of care.

Your body has shrunken
To skin over bone,
It won't be long now
Until you are gone.

Gone on to live
In that blessed place
Where sorrow is vanquished
And all tears erased.

This frail earthly body
Soon now you will shed
For the glorious new one
That waits just ahead.

Your work here
Is almost done,

Your final battle
Soon will be won.

Perhaps even before
This day is done,
Your final race
Will now be run.

You'll sleep to wake
On Heaven's bright shore,
Where tears and sorrow
And pain are no more.

Soon we will join you
In that promised land,
Oh precious reunion
To part not again!

For my father, *Emil Burgess*.

May 15, 1972

ODE TO SUMMER

It's hot as blue blazes
This much is true,
But at least we can go
Without coat or a shoe.

I'd rather be warm
Than bitterly cold;
I hate to wear clothes—
Even now that I'm old!

August 11, 2007

LIFE'S HIGHWAY

Sometimes you meet
On life's highway
Someone you know
Is a friend to stay.

Someone you know
Right from the start
Is destined to be
A friend of the heart.

A friend such as this
Is life's great treasure,
A friend you can't neglect
Or forget or measure.

You have been
This kind of friend;
I hope our paths
Will soon cross again!

For *Elizabeth Jackson*

December 3, 1999

CROSSROADS

Sometimes in life
On a given day,
You meet another
On life's highway.

Sometimes you'll know
With just a glance,
This meeting was not
Just by some chance.

A time to learn
From one another
That all can live
As sister or brother.

A time to learn,
A time to know
That sharing with others
Is how we grow.

If you are open,
And if you dare,

So many things
You two can share.

If the book is open,
You can turn the page;
Kindred spirits from
Any creed, race, age.

Common interests, ideas,
Dreams, aspirations—
A sharing of thoughts
Gives each inspiration.

The road takes a turn,
Each goes their own way;
Perhaps their paths'll
Cross another day.

For my very young friend, *Chondra Carston.*

November 7, 1996

LADY DEL

A woman for all times,
And for all seasons,
A citizen of the world
For memorable reasons.

A lady who's endured
A great many things,
Yet feels right at home
With presidents and kings.

In the land of Belgium,
When she was just three,
Her family's great danger
Forced them to flee.

Escaping persecution
On the ship called *Lorraine*,
Leaving their homeland
To return ne'er again.

Landing in New York
On that great steamship,

So lucky they were
To give Nazis the slip.

Her loving father,
A tailor by trade,
Sought help in Dakota—
Her family found aid.

So they were settled
In our great land,
Went to California,
Where she met her man.

Lady Del and beloved Bud
Between them raised three good sons
And those three had more in turn—
So many, many little ones!

Her family's gone this way and that,
And now she lives alone,
With Li'l Ruth her constant friend,
Now that Bud is gone.

What a wondrous life,
So much to tell,
All those who love her
Now wish her well!

For *Del Castor* on her ninety-second birthday,
December 31, 2007.
(Ruth is her beloved little dog.)

DID YOU KNOW?

At the end of the road
Next to the railroad track,
Each day I saw your home
As I went to work and back.

A modest dwelling,
This place you called home;
Each year I saw changes;
Soon you were gone.

Scrub bushes and jonquils,
A chinaberry tree,
A wide front porch,
Not much else to see.

One day I noticed
Your truck was gone.
I saw a wheelchair ramp,
Both wide and long.

One day I noticed
No lights were on;

The ramp had been moved—
I knew you were gone.

Not long thereafter
Your house was torn down—
Gone a lifetime of memories,
Leaving bare empty ground.

I passed by one day
In early spring,
And saw big tractors
As they were plowing.

That summer the farmer
Had a good yield
From your old home place—
Now a cotton field.

All that is left
Of your place, I see,
Is a few scrub bushes—
And a chinaberry tree.

May 20, 2001

FOREVER FRIENDS

So many memories
Of days long gone;
I still love you,
Each and every one.

You were my first
And dearest friends;
That kind of friendship
Just never ends.

I can still see us
Sitting at our desks,
Someone peeking over
As we were taking tests.

All through high school
We were the smallest class;
Many of us dirt-poor—
But we had a blast!

Covering for each other,
Looking back it seems,

Whatever came up,
We were a team.

We were so young,
Just beginning in life;
Since then we've had
Many struggles and strife.

To those gone before,
Soon we will follow too;
Be watching for us,
We'll be looking for you!

For the 1955 Senior Class of Rayville High School,
Rayville, Louisiana

October 29, 2010

NEW LIGHT BAPTIST CHURCH

One hundred years ago
This sparsely settled tier
Had no school or church
Anywhere even near.

The god-fearing settlers
Took matters into hand,
And chartered them a church
On donated land.

Beside the red school house,
In a humble arbor,
Banding folks together,
They found a safe harbor.

Can you just see them,
Off to church or to school,
Or riding in a wagon,
Pulled by horse or mule?

Wearing sun bonnets
And long-flowing tresses,
Buttoned-up shoes,
And most modest dresses.

So much of our past
Remains a mystery;
We wish we knew more
Of our Church history!

From humble beginnings
New light has come to be—
A beacon of hope
In our community.

Our Church on the corner
Will continue to be
A place of refuge
Where we worship free.

One-hundredth birthday homecoming, New Light Baptist Church, 1910-2010

July 25, 2010

DARKNESS TO LIGHT

Sky black as midnight,
Everything was so dim,
All was in darkness,
The Father couldn't look at Him.

He could not watch Him
Endure such agony,
As Christ bore our sins
On Mount Calvary.

His tender flesh macerated
Where He was flayed,
Hanging in strips
Where the lashes were laid.

His precious dear body
Exposed naked in shame
This Holy One of God
Named o'er every name.

Imagine every vile thought
And evil deed every done

All heaped and piled
On God's only Son.

He went there by choice,
A sacrifice He chose to be,
To secure salvation
For you and for me.

April 10, 2009

TELL ME THE STORY

As told from days of old,
In the town of Bethlehem
They say a King was born—
Somehow I know it was Him!

In a lowly manger
Filled up with hay,
The King of Glory
Was laid down that day.

No place was prepared
For His long-'waited birth,
The One who'd someday
Rule the earth.

He made his dwelling
Here among men;
Our Creator came
To save us from sin.

So now as we give gifts
To friends and to kin,

Let us remember
A gift for him!

December 24, 2009

SIGNS AND WONDERS

Found swaddled in a stable
Among animals and hay,
The great King of Glory
Came to us that day.

Did the animals draw near
To look upon His face?
God's Glory come down
To save Adam's race.

Did they speak softly to Him,
And welcome the new King;
Were the shepherds in awe
To hear the angels sing?

Wise men were on their way
From distances so far,
In search of their Savior,
They followed His star.

Amidst signs and wonders
The star came to stay,

And stood still above
The place where He lay.

To find the new King
At the time of His birth,
Wise men sought Him then
From the ends of the earth.

Wise men sought Him then,
Although they were few;
Down through the ages
Wise men still do!

December 19, 2009

TELL ME AGAIN

On Easter morning
Seems everyone knows,
We must go to church
And wear our new clothes.

Dressed up in our finest
We fill up the pews,
We've come again
To hear the good news.

How the tomb was empty
Where Jesus did lay;
He was not there
That break of day.

We come to hear
His story again,
How He came to earth
To redeem man.

Death could not hold
The Father's own Son,

He conquered the grave,
God's Holy One.

April 4, 2010

FOR THE CHILD WHO REMEMBERS

My heart is broken
To see your tears,
Learn of your sorrow
Down through the years.

You've suffered what no one
Should have to go through;
My heart is broken
For the younger you.

No child should have
To suffer such pain,
Abuse, and neglect,
Not ever again.

What can I do?
I cannot erase
The horrors you were dealt
By depraved human race.

There's no way to describe
The anger I feel
For your neglect
By another's will.

Just know that I care,
Though I never knew
The anguish you felt
When no one helped you.

November 28, 2007

EMERGENCY!!!

I always come here
When I have a great need;
You'll listen with care,
My concerns you'll heed.

This time when I came
My heart was racing away;
I really wasn't sure
I'd see another day.

What's your problem?
Someone did ask. I said,
"Tachycardia—two hours!"—
Y'all threw me in bed!

I think the whole staff
Converged on my room—
That'll give some thoughts
Of possible doom!

"No 'P' waves,"
I heard the doctor say;

That gave me pause
At start of day.

"Too fast to tell!"
I heard Doc mutter;
Then—"I see it now!
"It's definitely flutter!"

"Now it's junctional,
"Now flutter, then fib!"
At this point I said,
"Don't press on my rib!"

"Osteoporosis
"Is not friendly to me:
"I'm very fragile,
"I break easily!"

Then my dear doctor
Said with sincerity:
"I have to stop your heart"—
Yes, he said that to me!

What? Stop my heart?
Such troubles I've got—
"You want to stop my heart?
"For real? Say what?"

Those E.R. nurses
Were all primed and ready

Whatever there came,
Their hands were steady.

Dear Doctor Davis,
And the E.R. crew,
Just want you to know,
I respect and love you!

To Dr. Randy Davis and all the St. Francis Medical Center Emergency Room staff, Monroe, Louisiana: Thanks, guys! You'll pulled me out again!

March 23, 2009

THE EXODUS

It's just three A.M.,
All the patients are asleep,
When Travis makes his rounds,
There's not even a peep.

But what's this I hear?
Gramps has gotten loose,
He's coming in here,
Naked as a plucked goose!

He motions to me
Where I lie in my bed:
"We're leaving now!"
And he runs on ahead.

Waving his foley bag
Overhead like a sword,
Riding his IVAC,
And dragging the cord!

This one is crazy,
To myself I said,

As I gingerly eased out
Of my own hospital bed.

Travis and Glenda
Are both down the hall,
And Marilyn's gone
On a "nature's call."

"It's now or it's never,"
I heard old Gramps say;
"Nurse Higgins'll be here
"At first break of day!"

Gramps and I take our time
In our run for the door,
To enlighten and rescue
Two or three more!

Dragging my chest tubes,
And a big IVAC too,
I can't find my robe,
I can't find a shoe.

I know me and Gramps
Are surely a sight,
In our mad dash for freedom
In the midst of the night.

If sickness doesn't kill you,
The treatment surely will:

Can't take another shot,
Can't take another pill!

Nurses, we love you: two
Debs and Lamonica too,
Pam, Ricky, and Jeannie,
To name just a few.

Jessie and Laverne,
We'll really miss you,
And Donna and Angie,
And sweet Beth too.

You're all such nice folks,
So how can you stay
In this chamber of torture,
For day after day?

Wait! Gramps and I know
Just what we must do:
In our rush toward freedom,
We'll take you, too!

With love and thanks to the Six West staff, St. Francis Medical Center, Monroe, Louisiana, especially Dr. Robert Marshall, Dr. Ron Hammett, Dr. Antti Maran, and the other physicians who attended me.

REFLECTIONS

Birds flying,
Moon rising.

Sun setting,
Planes jetting.

Cool breezes,
Ocean spray.
Red purple skies,
End of day.

Tides rushing in
With a shout;
Then silently
Flowing out.

Songbirds a-winging
On their way;
Winds a-singing
This cloudy day.

Fresh-plowed earth
Rivers and fountains;

Double rainbows,
Hilltops and mountains.

Earthly loved ones,
Family and friends;
I'll miss most of all,
When my journey ends.

September 30, 1995

PO', PO' ME!

My ears are on crooked,
My brain is fried,
I can't remember my name,
I'm fit to be tied.

Can anyone tell me
Just who I am?
If I could stay on my feet,
I'd go on the lam!

My brain is addled—
Don't be amused!
I wish I could help it—
I'm just so confused.

I cannot remember
If I have eaten;
My entire body feels
Like it's been beaten.

So please come get me
Before they haul me away;

I can't stand this confusion
Even one more day!

Have I had lunch?
I can't really say;
I know I ate tuna—
Or was that yesterday?

I stand at the sink
And contemplate my toes
Why I came in here,
Only heaven knows!

Is it time for bed,
Or did I just get up,
Time to cook supper,
Or time to wash up?

If anyone knows,
Please give me a clue;
I can't remember your name,
But I'm counting on you!

April 26, 2004

REMEMBER WHEN?

All you had to fear
Was catching the dread "itch,"
Or seeing horrid troll
Lurking down in the ditch,
Or hiding 'neath the bridge
From the fiery dragon
Coming o'er the next ridge?

Oh, to go back to those days,
The days of our youth,
When we were all free,
And seeking the truth.
We heard the old tales
As we worked in the field;
We shivered a bit,
But knew they weren't real!

We had good neighbors
Who all felt like kin;
Oh, just for a day,
To go back to then!

May 5, 2010

ARLIN CARR

It's hard to believe
What I've been told:
That you are now
Eighty years old!

But just you wait—
Let me bite my tongue!
I should have said:
Eighty years young!

Well, I must say
Your age doesn't show:
To me you look like
You did thirty years ago!

So much you have given
While here on earth;
Only God knows
What a life is worth.

When I look back,
I can clearly see

You and your brothers
At the Ward Five Jamboree.

You shared your gift;
Many came from far and near,
Just for the pleasure
Of your music to hear.

Be sure your talent
Will follow after you;
So many of your offspring
Can play and sing, too!

Your legacy lives on—
I cannot measure
To how many lives
Your music gave pleasure.

So, happy birthday, dear friend!
We wish you many more;
We'll be looking for you
To reach five score!

May 24, 2004

SENIOR CITIZENS

Old age is not for sissies,
I've often heard them say;
We offer living proof
On our special day.

We've survived bouts of cancer,
Heart attacks and flu,
Open-heart surgery,
To name but a few.

We've had our hearts stopped
To slow them down,
While everyone prayed,
We've come back around.

We can't jump out of bed,
But are more likely to creep;
We often stop breathing
As we snore in our sleep!

But still we are here,
Though aging in years;

We still love laughter,
And we still shed tears.

So don't you forget
That we're people too;
Only difference is:
We're older than you!

February 17, 2010

BE MERCIFUL

Each one of us,
In our own way,
In quiet desperation
Meet each new day.

Each one of us
Has burdens to bear;
Every one of us
Needs someone to care.

So often we carry
A very large load,
Burdened down with care
To the end of the road.

So let us be kind
Each to the other;
Treat each as though
A sister or brother.

Though loads get heavy,
As they sometimes do,

I wouldn't swap any
Of my problems with you.

Yours are much worse,
That's easy to see:
So I'm happy to keep
Those entrusted to me.

June 24, 2007

NOT TO BE

It has been so hard
From you to part;
I carried you in
And under my heart.

I so regret
Your life won't be;
You were formed
From part of me.

I know you must go,
I can't accept it yet;
Our parting has come
With such deep regret.

I know I will always
Shed bitter tears;
Each year on this day,
Down through the years.

Your life was taken
Ere it got its start,

But you will always live
Deep within my heart.

For all those who lost their unborns.

April 17, 1997

BIRTHDAY REFLECTION

I really don't need
Pricey gifts from the store;
I have friends and family—
I can't ask for more.

Everything that I need
To enjoy life and living,
To be blessed and be happy,
I have been given.

March 6, 2006

STORMS OF LIFE

No one can know,
No one can see
Why so many things
Like this must be.

Sometimes all you can do
Is go with the flow,
Until the storm passes—
And it will, you know!

In the meantime,
Just hold your head high,
Soon it'll be better,
When the storm passes by.

August 30, 2001

SUMMER DANCE

Sweet summer's breeze,
Waltzing in,
Mimosas dancing
In the wind.

New tender branches
Dipping down,
Bowing gently
To kiss the ground.

Lifting, swirling,
Turning around,
With lilting, joyful,
Whispering sound.

July, 1985

FAMILY TREE

As you start to climb
Your family tree,
Perhaps you'll find
You're related to me!

Sometimes we'll find
Just ifs, ands, and buts,
An outlaw or two,
And even some nuts.

Don't be discouraged
They're out there somewhere,
Or else we're descended
Whole from thin air!

Sometimes I think
Old wives' tales were true:
'Twas in the cabbage patch
They found me and you!

August 22, 2006

SUGAR

Deep in my heart,
Today I cried,
When you called to say
That Sugar had died.

She was such a sweet,
Good-natured girl;
Her spirit's now gone
Out of this world.

Your beautiful filly
Runs here no more;
But I believe she now runs
Along Heaven's bright shore.

You'll always miss her,
This much I can say;
She waits there for you
To join her someday.

She loved her family,
And we loved her too;

Her favorite person
In the whole world was you.

I believe she will watch,
And she'll stand and wait,
To see if you're coming
To the fence or the gate.

For Kalyn Carr, who loved her beautiful paint, Sugar.

January 26, 2008

CLASSMATES AND FRIENDS

There's a bond that exists
Amongst friends of our youth,
From early in life
We shared pain and truth.

Those who loved us first,
We'll remember forever;
There's a heart connection
No one can sever.

We shared so much
That time can't erase;
In my mind I can see
Each dear, loving face.

And if by chance
I see you nevermore,
I'll wait there for you
On that beautiful shore.

For classmates, kin, and friends, Rayville High School, Rayville, Louisiana, *January 11, 2008*

CHILDREN OF THE WORLD

To all the dear children
Here and everywhere,
We want you to know
we remember and care.

Many of you ask
Very little of life:
Family and friends,
And freedom from strife.

Food, shelter, clothing,
A roof overhead,
Enough to eat,
And a safe, warm bed.

For each of you
These things we pray:
God's richest blessings
Each and every day.

So, Christmas children:
To show we care,

This small gift's for you,
Filled with love and care.

For Samaritan's Purse Christmas Shoeboxes.

THIS DAY

It seems like forever,
Yet only yesterday,
When I lost my Daddy,
Thirty-two years ago today.

Forever and always
His memory lives on,
So hard to believe
He truly is gone.

My Daddy was special,
He was always kind;
To us and to others,
He was truly fine.

He worked very hard
All of his life;
His struggles were many:
He endured such strife.

He was a man of honor,
Known far and wide

For his generous nature,
Taking the underdog's side.

He taught by example
The things we should know,
Always pointing out
The way we should go.

He lives in my heart,
And walks close to me;
Someday I'll join him
For all eternity.

In memory of *Emil Burgess*,
August 14, 1901-May 3, 1972

May 3, 2004

THE JOURNEY

Like ships that pass
Each other at night,
Too soon the sails
Are lost from sight.

The secret of life
Lies in the knowing
From whence you came,
And where you are going.

So remember these words,
As you travel on:
His angels are guiding;
You are not alone!

September 19, 1996

FOR MY CAREGIVER

I loved you so
Right from the start;
I carried you in
And under my heart.

I tended your needs
With love and with care;
I cleaned your body
And combed your hair.

Each day I gave
Your daily bread,
Cleaned your clothes,
And made your bed.

Now I am old
And helpless too;
So now I must
Depend on you.

I gave to you
My very best.

Now for me
Will you do less?

September 15, 1997

METAMORPHOSES

Often times in this life
The body is weary and worn,
The soul imprisoned
In a shell that is torn.

We weep and we cry
As eternity draws nigh
While our loved one
Prepares to die.

The cocoon shatters,
It falls away,
The butterfly emerges
To start a new day.

So now they are free,
Truly free at last,
As the outer shell
Aside is cast.

January 17, 2005

MOTHER'S DAY

Today as we remember
Those who gave us birth,
Who loved us best
Of all who live on earth.

There's simply no way
We could ever repay
The dear ones we honor
On this special day.

Flesh of her flesh,
Bone of her bone:
The depth of her giving
Known to God alone.

If we stop to reflect
It's easy to see:
A mother's love extends
Throughout eternity.

May 11, 2008

REMEMBER THIS DAY

Throughout your life
As you go on your way,
You will remember
This special day.

So wherever you go,
And whatever you do,
Just want you to know,
I'm proud of you!

May God bless you
Each hour of the day;
His angels watch o'er you
Each step of the way.

For Justin Adam Carr on his high school graduation.

May 3, 2008

STARSHINE

He was born under
A great shining star;
Worshippers came
From near and from far.

Born was a babe,
The hope of mankind,
In a humble manger
Lit by starshine.

Born in a stable
Near the lowly sod,
He was truly man,
Yet truly God.

Sent to us
By His Father above:
The greatest of all
Gifts of love.

December 25, 2009

A BEND IN THE ROAD

So many changes
We face in our life:
Some are of pleasure,
Others full of strife.

We cannot sit still,
Life keeps running past;l
We must catch ahold,
And follow to the last.

We each are made up
Of all that came before;
Each new experience
Opens another door.

So, as we travel
Along to road's end,
We may find something better
Just 'round the next bend!

For Sandy Hammett

September 16, 2004

ADAMS FAMILY REUNION 2004

Adams and Neals
Woodells and Byrds,
Friends and others
Will be there, I've heard.

So, I wish I could join you,
To me you are dear;
Perhaps, God willing,
Will see you next year.

If we meet not again
Here on this side,
We'll meet once more
When the doors open wide.

And when we meet
On that eternal shore,
Our elusive ancestors
Will be strangers no more.

Then we will know,
As we are known here:
Such a joyous reunion,
With constant good cheer!

BURGESS REUNION 2001

Life moves so swiftly,
So soon are we gone,
Leaving others to grieve,
And to carry on.

Each of us has troubles
And trials, I find,
But I wouldn't trade any
Of yours for mine!

Each of us is given
Our very own share
Of struggles and worries
And burdens to bear.

We each leave footprints
In the sands of time,
A legacy to others,
Our gift to mankind.

Let's stop to think
Of the things that we say;

Remember those who follow
Us along life's highway!

Richland Parish, Louisiana.

June 20, 2001

A WALK IN LIFE

He followed you
Just a step behind;
You always knew
You were on his mind.

You taught him how
To hunt and fish,
To be just like you
Was his greatest wish.

He trusted in you
As he did no other;
To him you were
His "older brother."

He became your conscience,
As you were his guide;
He always tried to
Walk closely by your side.

See what you've wrought
In this fine gentle man,

For you can take credit
Where few others can.

You sowed good seed:
See how he's grown,
In quiet strength and courage
From seeds you have sown.

You gave him guidance
When he needed you,
And when you grew tired,
He carried you through.

Together for always,
You are brothers in love,
As you each follow
Your Father above.

For my nephews, Michael Linder and Robbie Carr.

August 9, 1989

TINA'S SWEATSHOP

Six or seven sewing machines
Line up in a row,
Each manned by a lady,
Ready and willing to sew.

Twenty-one angel costumes,
Choir vestures new;
Shawls for the wise men,
Joseph and Mary too.

Great bolts of red flannel,
Broadcloths of white
Silver sequined metallics
To capture the light.

Each person present,
There for one reason:
To make ready the garments
For this Christmas season.

We all put in such
Long hours of work;

We pulled together,
And not one did shirk.

Our feet were sore,
And that's a fact!
And not one of us
Escaped an aching back.

Our knees would buckle,
Crackle, and pop,
Until someone would say,
"We really have to stop!"

But Roy was in the kitchen,
A real handy man:
He really has a way
With the pot and the pan.

Cake, salad, cornbread,
A big pot of soup:
A real welcome treat
For our weary group.

Tina, Reba, Kathy, Ann,
Sheila and Peggy too,
Mildred, Mary, and Lynn,
We all counted on you.

You can be proud
Of what you have done

The committee thanks you,
Each and every one!

October 15, 2006

ANNIVERSARY CELEBRATION

You've been together
These past forty years,
Sharing good times and bad,
And laughter and tears.

You raised five children
Until they were grown,
And then pretty soon
Seven grandkids came 'long.

You've enjoyed each one,
Each one is a treasure:
They've given you joy
That is beyond measure.

Times weren't always easy,
Sometimes times were sad,
But you weathered the storm
Through good times and bad.

You added more branches
To our family tree:

A great addition
To the Burgess fam'ly.

Our parents were proud
Of all you have done,
And they dearly loved
Their daughter and son.

A sister we gained
Without losing our brother;
To be in our family,
We'd want no other.

Brother, you chose
A very good wife
To walk beside you
On the pathway of life.

Congrats to you both
This anniversary day:
God bless and keep you,
The rest of life's way!

Jessie Mae Hamm & Robert S. Burgess, Sr.
August 7, 1958-August 7, 1998

MEMORIES

In the course of my work as a nurse, I encountered many individuals, old and young, who simply didn't "make it." Some of these folks were poor, or had few friends or relatives—and so I started writing these bits of verse to commemorate their passing. Later I added remembrances of the deaths of too many friends and acquaintances of my own.

DONALD WHITE

A blessed relief
From torment and pain,
All sorrow will cease
As Heaven you gain.

Freedom to run,
Freedom to play,
Freedom to stand,
And to walk this day.

You're no longer bound
By a body of clay;
You're free now to soar
Into a bright new day.

Faith, love, and courage
Reigned in your life
Through many dangers
Amidst great strife.

You gave all you had,
Always did your best,

And you trusted in Him
To do all the rest.

A special young man, a scholar, a man of integrity who had insurmountable health problems—he will be sorely missed.

March 18, 1995

DOYLE E. GREEN, SR.

This one was special,
One of the best;
His life here is over,
He's gone to his rest.

I can still see him
In those blue overalls,
Milking those cows
In the dairy stalls.

He lived very close
To the soil and the earth,
Never moving too far
From the place of his birth.

So early in life
He suffered great pain:
Both parents gone
To return ne'er again.

His family asunder,
Scattered everywhere;

It was so hard,
It didn't seem fair.

He made the best of
This great tragedy,
Marrying and raising
His own family.

He had all he needed
To be happy in life:
Three great kids,
And a dear loving wife.

Now he can stand,
Even run and play:
The shackles that bound him
Were loosened today!

In loving memory of my dear cousin, *"Bubba" Green*
June 27, 1943-October 11, 2007

ISAAC HARRIS

A loving husband
And father now gone,
Leaving his loved ones
Who must carry on.

He lived a good
And upright life;
Always he treasured
His dear sweet wife.

Always were honored
The vows that were said.
The marriage license, framed,
Hung over their bed.

They never attained
Any worldly wealth,
But they stood together
Through sickness and health.

He gladly left off
His frail body of clay,

Moved onward and upward
To a bright shining day.

Like a bright butterfly
Just taking to wing,
Now he has flown
To where angels sing.

October 25, 1936-January 29, 1998

REV. LINDLE STEWART

Pastor, teacher,
Leader, friend,
One who sticks
To the bitter end.

Even near the end,
He's always there,
Our sorrow, pain,
And grief to share.

He walks with us
As we go through life,
Upheld, supported
By his own dear wife.

He leads by example
The sheep in his fold;
The reach of his arms
Can never be told.

For our pastor, his wife Yvonne, and their family.

October 2009

ZELMA THOMPSON

"I'm going home!
"Home for Christmas!" she said.
"But I'm so tired"—
Couldn't raise her head.

"I'm going to see my mama,
"Going to see my 'Little Man'"
(Her husband who died last year.)
"I can't wait to see my Sallie again."

She said, "I'm ready,"
"I'm anxious to go,
"There to be united
"With those I love so."

"So tired and weary
"Of suffering and pain,
"With nothing to lose,
"But Heaven to gain."

Where, o death, is your victory,
Where is your sting?

She joyfully left this earth—
The angels did sing!

December 18, 1995

MOTHER ROBERTA COLEMAN

"Don't be crying for me,"
I can hear her say.
"Child, don't you know?
"It's my graduation day!

"When you needed anything,
"You called on me, dear;
"And through the long years
"I was always there.

"By loving example
"I showed you the way:
"How to work hard,
"And how to pray.

"I took you to church,
"And to sunday school;
"I taught you good manners,
"And the golden rule.

"In this present existence
"That we call life,
"So often we struggle
"With troubles and strife.

"My testing is over,
"My life here's ending,
"My race is now won,
"Eternity's beckoning!"

October 18, 1910-August 28, 2001

BILL "PUTT" LINDER

I look for you
Where you're no more;
Your seat stays empty
At the one-stop store.

A friend to all
You served so well;
The good you've done
No man can tell.

Why such a man
Was shot down in his prime,
We cannot know
At this place in time.

Is there no place
Left on this earth,
Where life's held dear
And accorded its worth?

All your friends
From far and near

Will cherish your memory,
And hold it dear.

You had to make
The great sacrifice,
Leaving a daughter,
A much beloved wife.

You laid your life down,
You gave all you could give,
You put yourself forward
So others would live.

Go now in peace
With your soul at rest,
Knowing that you gave
Always your best.

Deputy Sheriff killed in the life of duty.

October 10, 2004

SAM NICKLEBERRY

Always searching for you
Through the mists of time,
Always hoping some trace
Of you we will find.

Sold at the end
Of the great Civil War,
Lost to your family
All scattered a-far.

We cannot know
All you went through,
Down through the years
We remember you.

We've searched for you
With bitter tears,
But no trace could be found
For a hundred years.

From Texas to Oakland
Your descendants came

And settled all over
Still bearing your name.

Your progeny multiplied
Like grains of sand;
Each one we meet's
An upstanding woman.

Your great-great-granddaughter
Only just recently
By chance met one
From the same family tree.

Another was found
At the corner store,
Rekindling fond dreams
Of finding much more.

One's package was lost,
But he crowed just the same:
For he met yet another
With the family name.

In this earthly life
We don't understand
How one can mistreat
His own fellowman.

Someday we will gather
At Heaven's front door

Reunited at last
To part nevermore!

Born 1858, died June 1944.

July 22, 1989

BARBARA MAXWELL BRANDIN

So softly and quietly
You slipped away,
Discarding and shedding
Your body of clay.

Leaving as you lived,
Without fuss or fanfare,
Looking for loved ones
Waiting you there!

Among precious memories
I know that will last
Was a very special member
Of our sunday school class.

We'll not meet here again,
We'll see you here no more;
But we know we'll yet meet
On Heaven's bright shore.

May 5, 2010

ALICE BADGER DAVIS

Born of another time,
Born in another place,
Accustomed to quietness,
And open country space.

Special parents she had,
A great father and mother
Each "one of a kind,"
She'd have no other.

The eldest of five,
So early in life,
She learned how to deal
With struggle and strife.

She took care of others,
Till the end of her days,
With no gain for her,
She never sought praise.

When her own health failed,
When she couldn't sustain,

She continued to labor
In spite of great pain.

Her troubles are over,
All sorrow is past;
Now she's at peace,
She's found rest at last.

July 18, 1918-October 3, 1998

JAMES BARNES

On your earthly journey
As the end was drawing near,
We watched the bright leaves
Becoming withered and sere.

Your light too soon left us
In your dwelling below;
It now joyfully burns
In Heaven's bright glow.

Your memory will always
Be precious and dear,
A remembered treasure
For loved ones here.

As they slip your remains
'Neath the brown, waiting sod,
Farewell, James Barnes:
Go now with God!

November 11, 1924-March 15, 2009

WILLIAM HUNTER CARR

A precious young man
Not yet fully grown;
Anyone would be proud
To call you their own.

In your young life
You brought such pleasure;
Your earthly road left
Such memories to treasure.

A precious son,
A beloved brother,
A loving offspring
To your own dear mother.

While you were here
You took the chance,
You stepped forth
And you chose to dance.

July 8, 2009

SHIRLEY EVELYN MAYO SPARKS

The immortal spirit
Will live on always,
Created by God
At the beginning of days.

No more pain or sorrow,
When the body is shed,
Just peace and happiness
For her lie ahead.

I know Heaven's gates
Did open wide,
When she slipped over
To the other side.

She's gone on the path
On which we must go,
When we have finished
Our work here below.

She's gone on ahead
Preparing the way,
For others to follow
At the end of life's day.

November 1, 1916-October 2, 2004

IRBALEA BURGESS WILLIAMSON

No thoughts can express,
No words can convey
The loss in our lives
As she left us this day.

But Heaven rejoiced,
Saying, "Come, come here!"
Her loved ones were waiting
That held her so dear.

Can you just imagine
So many to greet her,
So many who cared
As they came to meet her.

Her own precious daughter,
Her parents so dear,
Her sister and brother,
All gone on from here.

I believe I can hear
"Welcome home, well done,
"Come now and rest,
"Your race is run."

I believe she could hear
The angel choirs sing,
As she safely crossed over
To her Savior and King.

For my dear cousin, who was like a sister to my orphaned mother, Nellie Elizabeth Green, when Irbalea's parents, Lucy Hixon and Grover Burgess, took Mama in.

October 13, 1928-May 18, 2009

SISTER ROSA CHEFFIN

Perhaps we should
Rejoice this day:
Our sister has
Gone home to stay.

As her earthly sight
Grew strangely dim,
She raised her arms,
And welcomed Him.

We would not wish
Her longer to remain,
Distressed and weary,
Wracked up with pain.

She sits at the feet
Of our Savior and King,
Giving praise unto Him
Where angels sing.

May 24, 1926-September 13, 1997

BROTHER GUS DAVIS

He was a gentleman
So full of trust,
A friend to all,
Called "Papa Gus."

He'd greet you with
A great big smile,
Saving, "Come on in,
"Rest your feet for a while."

The end of each day
Found him weary and tired;
You couldn't keep him out
Of his garden and yard.

Each summer he was
In his finest hours,
Showing off his plants,
His famous sunflowers.

Gus didn't have
A real easy life:

He had to bury
Four sons and his wife.

With ninety-eight years,
He felt he was blessed,
Before he entered
His eternal rest.

October 9, 1898-February 27, 1997

BROTHER EMEAL PRICE

This dear sweet man,
So soon gone away,
Will always be missed
Each and every day.

A man of few words
Known for his kind heart
And gentle, caring spirit,
He always did his part.

To help make the world
Into a much better place,
Upholding and uplifting
The entire human race.

It's good to celebrate
A well-lived life,
Full of peace and love,
Not marred by strife.

Always remember,
Now that he's gone,

His gentle caring spirit
Will still live on.

June 28, 1917-May 27, 2001

ED SINGLETON

A very special man
Left us this day,
When God looked down,
And called him away.

No more rooting flowers,
Or mowing the lawn,
Don't look for him:
Our Mr. Ed is gone.

He did not awaken
From a nap so deep;
He slipped away
Silently in his sleep.

Many things we remember
About this special man
A wonderful smile,
A ready, helping hand.

The things he enjoyed
In his earthly life:

His dear children,
His loving wife.

Ed lived a good life
Right to the very end;
Farewell and Godspeed,
Dear neighbor and friend!

June 28, 2007

VERNIE BYNOG

We do not know,
We cannot say,
Why she was taken
From us this day.

We can only trust
In Our Father above,
Knowing His precious
And unending love.

She is at rest,
All pain is past,
With joy and peace,
She's home at last!

Don't weep wild tears
For her—no way!
For surely you know
It's her graduation day!

May 22, 2007

ALVERNE TELANO BAMBURG

From long earthly days,
She's gone now to rest,
Forever and always,
To dwell with the blest.

Now seem too few
Her days here below;
You wanted her to stay,
But she had to go!

Her struggles and trials
Are all now past;
She's freed from all sorrow,
She's home at last!

Somehow I feel
She always knew
This wasn't her home—
Just passing through!

She made the safe passage
Surrounded by love,
As she crossed over
To her Father above.

She will be missed
Forever and always;
Her memory will remain
With you all your days.

May 28, 2007

BROTHER GEORGE MILLS

"A good neighbor."
"He'd lend a hand."
"A 'people' person."
"A man's man."

"That man stored many
"Facts in his head."
"The best teacher I ever had."
These were the things they said!

A lover of life
Whose interests were many—
Community, education, sports,
And friends a-plenty.

They say he was always
In a good mood;
He loved conversation,
People and good food.

He was very active
In church and civic affairs,

Lifting up others
Out of life's cares.

He said he was ready:
His body was worn;
Ninety-five good years
With no reason to mourn.

"Ready, I'm ready,"
The last words he said;
To life's next adventure
He forged right ahead.

He left praising God
For his good dear wife,
Singing glory and praises
For his long earthly life!

February 19, 1903-September 4, 1998

MARY LYNN TELANO PORTER

"Come on, come home,"
She heard Jesus say,
"Come home, my child,
"Come home today,

"Your work is done
"You were sent to do,
"So now hurry home:
"I am calling you!

"So many await you
"On Heaven's shore;
"Come rejoin them
"To part nevermore.

"Now you can see
"The white pearly gates;
"Come on, come home:
"For you Heaven waits!"

October 24, 2009

LILLIE BELL "GRANNY" GOINS

Like the loaves and fishes
That multiplied,
She fed the many
From meager supplies.

Of money she had none,
What she had she gave:
She put it on the line
Souls and bodies to save.

She forever will be known
As a friend to man;
She gave her all,
Her legacy will stand.

She started a soup kitchen for the needy.

JOSEPH POE

From West Alabama
There came a man
Unafraid to stand tall
Or take a stand.

A man with courage
To be all he could be:
An example to others
Of friends and family.

A very special man,
An enforcer of law,
A gentle family man,
As you all saw.

Respected and honored,
Not seeking fame,
Trustworthy, honest,
A man of good name.

We surely do hate
To see you go:

Godspeed, farewell,
Detective Joseph Poe.

September 20, 1996

CORPORAL CLOVIS WAYNE "J. R." SEARCY

A beloved public servant
One of the best,
Gone from us now
To his eternal rest.

A precious young man,
Cut down in his prime;
Who could have known
It had come your time?

A special young man,
Really one of a kind,
Always faithfully serving
With his trusty canine.

On that fateful day,
When you answered the call,
Of your partner in need
You gave your all.

We cannot know,
We cannot say,
Why you were taken,
That sad mournful day.

Even in death
You continued to give:
Your body was shared,
So others could live.

I think you can hear,
And I think that you know:
To so many here
You're our hero!

Killed in the line of duty.

March 6, 2010

RUBY NELL WOODS

She flew away
To Heaven at last;
All sorrow and pain
Are now in the past.

She is now free,
Her race is run:
A new life in glory
Has just begun.

We can imagine
Her having fun:
Now able to walk,
Now able to run.

Free from this mortal
Body of clay;
She's free at last,
She went home today.

July 11, 1939-October 11, 2000

VERA WILSON

You had to go,
You had no choice
Once you heard the call
Of your Savior's voice.

We do not know,
Nor can we understand
Why this was a part
Of His master plan.

God in His wisdom
Knows the reason
You had to face
This time and season.

Now your work
On earth is done;
You fought the good fight,
Your race is run.

She dropped dead carrying her baby at term.

June 26, 1997

AVERY WILSON

They tell me "Avery"
Is the name
Your mother gave you
Before you came.

You are a tiny
Baby boy
You'd have been
Her pride and joy.

She was struck down
Ere you were born,
On that strange and
Mournful, fateful morn.

For your life
She had great plans:
You would dream dreams
Would see distant lands.

All hopes and plans
Are gone astray;

Why this should be,
We cannot say.

Still, we must trust
In our Father above,
For we know his mercies,
His undying love.

His mother, Vera Wilson (see the preceding poem), died before her child was born; he was saved by emergency surgery.

June 26, 1997

ARLIN CARR

You said I should leave,
You said I must go,
But the note in my pocket
Said you still loved me so.

I left as you said,
And went on my way;
The note in my pocket
I found just today.

So troubled was the time
I spent with you;
Did you find my note
Saying, "I love you too"?

Never again
Will I see your face,
Here in this life,
In this time and place.

Now you are gone,
From troubles set free;

The note in my pocket
Is all you left me.

February 17, 2005

BENET SMITH

A good man,
A good life,
Supported by
A loving wife.

A country boy,
A rural youth
Reared by parents
Who taught him truth.

Simple things
You cannot measure;
Fishing and family
He did so treasure.

Reared as he was
Close to the sod,
Very early he learned
To trust in God.

Now he comes
Back home to rest,

Joining those
Who loved him best.

So now don't weep,
And shed those tears:
Just remember him
Down through the years.

October 26, 1942-October 23, 1998

REV. EUGENE MARTIN

Not just a leader,
He was a pioneer,
Championing the causes
All people hold dear.

On freedom and education
He set his sights;
He was at the forefront
For equal civil rights.

Ahead of his time,
He helped forge the way,
Always leading the cause
Into a new day.

He stood so tall,
A head above the rest,
To each dream of his heart
He gave his very best.

In addition to this,
Throughout his life,

He upheld family values
With his dear lovely wife.

Now they are united
In Heaven's fair land,
Where sickness and sorrow
Will not come again.

All earthly trials
Have been overcome:
His battles are over,
His long race is run.

August 31, 1913-August 24, 1998

ELIZABETH SLEDGE

You've gone on ahead
To where there's always room,
To visit loved ones
Where flowers always bloom.

You shared so many
Lovely plants here below,
In so many places
You left flowers to show.

Each time I see
The dew on the rose,
I'll remember your smile,
As you gave me those.

In this harsh world
You dared to care,
So you always had plenty
With others to share.

You left a memory
So sweet and so true:

Wherever flowers grow,
I'll e're think of you.

May 1, 1918-September 22, 1997

ALINE COLLIE

The immortal spirit
Will live always,
Created by God
At the beginning of days.

No more pain and sorrow
When the body is shed;
Just peace and hkappiness
For you lie ahead.

I know Heaven's gates
Will open wide,
When you slip over
To life's other side.

A heavenly crown
He will bestow,
On one who gave
So much here below.

So many loved ones—
Nanny, Dwight, Bitsey too—

Will be waiting and watching
To get a glimpse of you.

They'll run to greet you,
And you will run too,
When earthly trials
And troubles are through.

To one who always showed the light for others.

November 16, 2003

HOLLIS JOHNSON

He was a good man,
Shining like a beacon,
Serving God and others,
And his church as Deacon.

He reared his children
With dignity and love,
Always trusting in His
Heavenly Father above.

He was a family man:
He loved his wife,
Taking care of her
To the last breath of life.

He gave his all,
Withstood every test,
Always trusting that
A loving God knows best.

Loved ones will meet him
On Heaven's bright shore,

Where pain, sickness, sorrow
Will come nevermore.

June 11, 1932-March 17, 1998

BARBARA SUE HUMPHRIES ENGLISH

A lady of beauty
Who knew great love,
Who trusted always
Her Father above.

Somehow we know
That God's spirit can
Always be with
The spirit of man.

Who knows the blessings
That to her did flow,
To her soul and spirit,
All her days below.

We feel and trust
That even in her sleep,
Her Father was with her,
As her soul He did keep.

Of this we can be certain,
With no room for doubt:
She left here rejoicing,
Crying "Yes" with a shout!

August 25, 1941-January 10, 2009

FLOYD DAVIS

"They" said you were
Just lying there,
Couldn't move or talk,
Or even comb your hair.

"They" didn't know,
Nor could they see
Just how much
You meant to me.

"They" said your care
Was such a chore,
But I always wanted
To do much more.

I still remember
Our younger days,
Your lovely smile,
And winning ways.

Now you are free
From your body of pain;

Now you can stand
And walk again.

So, run on ahead,
I'll meet you there,
Where flowers bloom
And skies are fair.

Written for his sister, Shirley Williams.

April 13, 1995

THELMA MARTIN

Not one to sit
And drowse in the shade,
With hands outstretched,
Awaiting accolade.

You were always busy,
Unafraid to toil,
Awaiting the reaping,
As you tended the soil.

Hard work, strength, and valor,
Great vision and integrity,
Hope, love, and laughter,
Are your joint legacy.

If "All the world's a stage,"
Then you were the star:
Your example and teaching
Reached those near and far.

What a great performance
There was nothing to lack

In the final curtain
From the first act.

We deem it a privilege
To have sat in the front row,
To view the unfolding
Of your one-woman show.

To say we will miss you
Does inadquately express
Our feelings at the loss of
The friend we thought best.

For "Blue," on the occasion of the tenth anniversary of the Supreme Home Health Services, Monroe, Louisiana.

June 24, 1993

ELOIS SIMMONS

Citizen of the world,
At home anywhere,
With anyone:
She could be serious
And very "grown-up,"
Yet still have fun
Wherever she went.
She fit right in,
Whether with family
Or stranger or friend:
A woman grown,
Yet still a girl,
At peace, at home
Anywhere in this world.

She was only here
For a little while
To spread love and laughter:
A warm, friendly smile,
A life so short
As lifetimes run.
You'd have thought
Hers had just begun.

She leaves behind
Sister and mother,
A beautiful young son,
And so many other
Relatives and friends
Who so regret to see
Her journey end.

Perhaps someday
We'll understand
Man's inhumanity to man—
We can only trust
In God until then.

January 24, 1972-April 16, 1999
She was murdered; Elois was the beloved daughter of my friend, Elizabeth Jackson.

April 23, 1999

CLIFFORD THARP

When you came to church
One last time this Father's Day,
And walked your victory lap
To never again pass this way,

Did you know this was to be
Your final farewell
To friends and neighbors?
Could you tell?

Did you laugh inside, knowing
Your race here was ending:
Soon no more pit stops
For patching and mending.

You showed grace and valor
Throughout earthly strife;
You won fair and square
In your race through this life.

You "revved" up your engine,
And away you did go,

Leaving behind precious memories
For your loved ones below.

August 22, 1930-June 23, 2008

MYRTA REESE BURGESS AVANTS

This one was special,
She loved everyone:
The joy of her life,
Her dear precious sons.

I can still see her
When they were all young,
Playing and laughing,
And having great fun.

She was my cousin,
And one of my friends:
This heart connection
Just never ends!

In later years
We were apart,
But always she knew
She was in my heart.

She kept up with everyone,
This much we knew:
We'd get Myrt's call,
Saying, "I love you!"

A precious sweet spirit
Gone from us this day:
But precious memories
Will linger always.

December 7, 2010

THE YEAR OF
THE RABBIT

Some of you may remember that time back in the mid-1950s when the crops failed. It was a miserable year from start to finish. First we had floods, then drought, then more floods. The cotton and corn crops never had a chance.

Mama and Daddy, Nellie and Emil Burgess, were rent-farming on Mr. Braswell's place on the Burke Road. Now, rent-farming left a lot to be desired, but was a big step up from share-cropping on the "Mudline." The rent-farmer's first profit belonged to the landlord. He was paid first. The next went to Tallulah Loan to buy seeds for the next year's crop, and/or to pay for this year's seeds. After that, honest debts were paid, then staples were bought to carry us through the winter: a barrel of flour, a keg of meal, sacks of sugar, soda, baking powder, salt, and pepper. Most everything else we raised ourselves.

I've seen years my parents and five children "lived" on less than one hundred dollars. We didn't have to worry about gas or electric bills or other such luxuries, as they were still in the future for us. In the particular year of which we speak, we "scrapped" the cotton several times to get two or three bales of poor quality cotton. This was our only livelihood for the year.

That year the Lord blessed us with an abundance of rabbits in the fields: truly manna from Heaven! Mama learned to cook rabbit in countless ways. We had it fried, baked, stewed, boiled, and roasted. She even made dumplings with them.

I wondered back then if everyone was as tired of rabbit as we were. I though surely the Burroughs, McGlothlins, and Normans in their big homes were eating better than we were.

One day after church, Fred and Kazee Norman invited me home with them for dinner. You can be sure I jumped at the opportunity. When we sat down for lunch, Kazee proudly said, "Lorene, I've got something really special for today. I know you will enjoy it!"

"Good," I replied, "I'm so sick of rabbit!" (My mouth always did get me into trouble!)

Kazee said, "Well, you'll like the way I fixed it. I've learned how to make rabbit salad!"

I said: "Kazee, Mama figured that out last week!"

We laughed till we cried, but she was right—I did like it!

I ran into Kazee at the Bend of the River Restaurant in Alto, Louisiana, about five years ago. We had another good laugh about "The Year of the Rabbit."

Monroe, Louisiana, 2001

INDEX OF POEMS

Adams Family Reunion 2004, 194
Adams Reunion, 41
Alice Badger Davis, 224
Aline Collie, 262
Alverne Telano Bamburg, 240
Anniversary Celebration, 203
Arlin Carr, 167, 254
Autumn, 45
Autumn Clouds, 82
Autumn Glory, 31
Avery Wilson, 252
Barbara Maxwell Brandin, 223
Barbara Sue Humphries English, 266
Be Merciful, 171
Beloved Mother, 119
A Bend in the Road, 193
Benet Smith, 256
Bill "Putt" Linder, 218
Birthday Reflection, 175
Boo, 102
Brother Emeal Price, 235
Brother George Mills, 242
Brother Gus Davis, 233
Burgess Reunion 2001, 196
Burgess Reunion 2010, 109

Camouflage, 37
Children of the World, 182
Classmates and Friends, 181
Choose Life, 86
Clifford Tharp, 274
Cloud on the Ground, 52
Coming Together, 116
Corporal Clovis Wayne "J. R." Searcy, 248
Crossroads, 136
Daddy, 118
Darkness to Light, 146
Day of Thanksgiving, 121
Did You Know?, 140
Donald White, 207
The Dove, 75
Doyle E. Green, Sr., 209
Dream of Another, 28
Dream Visits, 51
Eagle Flight, 77
Ed Singleton, 237
Elizabeth Sledge, 260
Elois Simmons, 272
Emergency!!!, 156
The Exodus, 159
Family Tree, 178
Fathers, 111
Fashion, 103
Fear Not, 88
Floyd Davis, 268
Fog, 46
For My Caregiver, 187
For the Child Who Remembers, 154
Forever Friends, 142
Freedom, 93
Guardian Angel, 76
Heart Attack at Thirty-Five, 126

The Heavens, 92
Hollis Johnson, 264
Home at Last, 64
Home Health Nurse, 132
I Want to Go Home, 39
In the Beginning, 113
Intensive Care, 101
Irbalea Burgess Williamson, 230
Isaac Harris, 211
It's the Living I'll Miss, 66
I've Heard It Said, 78
James Barnes, 226
Jim, 100
Joseph Poe, 246
The Journey, 186
Joyful Reunion, 18
Lady Del, 138
The Lamb, 74
Legacy, 54
A Legend in His Own Time, 26
Legendary Junior Collings, 43
Life's Highway, 135
Lillie Bell "Granny" Goins, 245
The Little Outhouse Out Back, 96
Look Around You, 129
Mama, 125
Mary Lynn Telano Porter, 244
Master Potter, 90
Memorial Day Remembrance, 123
Metamorphoses, 189
Millie the Spitz, 99
Missing You, 49
Mother, 22
Mother's Day, 190
Mother Roberta Coleman, 216

My Prayer, 104
Myrta Reese Burgess Avants, 276
New Light Baptist Church, 144
Not to Be, 173
Now, 95
A Nurse's Lament, 70
Ode to Summer, 134
Omen, 35
Our Family, 114
Po', Po' Me, 164
Precious Memories, 23
Reflections, 162
Reflections on All-Hallows Eve, 83
The Regal Pine, 32
Remember This Day, 191
Remember When?, 166
Remembrance, 13
Rev. Eugene Martin, 258
Rev. Lindle Stewart, 213
Ruby Nell Woods, 250
Sam Nickleberry, 220
Scribblings, 98
Seasons, 58
Senior Citizens, 169
She Sits and Waits, 57
Shirley Evelyn Mayo Sparks, 228
Signs and Wonders, 150
Sister Rosa Cheffin, 232
Starshine, 192
Storms of Life, 176
Sugar, 179
Summer Dance, 177
Sunset-Moonrise, 79
Tell Me Again, 152
Tell Me the Story, 148
Thelma Martin, 270

These I Have Seen, 34
This Day, 184
This Too Will Pass, 68
Tina's Sweatshop, 200
To One Grown Weary, 132
To One Who Has Crossed Over, 20
To Those Who Murder, 62
Trust Him, 91
An Ungrateful Lot, 60
Vera Wilson, 251
Vernie Bynog, 239
A Walk in Life, 198
What Then?, 47
Wherever Flowers Grow, 53
Who Am I?, 105
Why?, 107
William Hunter Carr, 227
Winter Rain, 56
Winter's Sculptures, 81
The Year of the Rabbit, 278
Your Faithful Friend, 67
Zelma Thompson, 214

ABOUT THE AUTHOR

I have been writing verses as long as I can remember, most of which are now lost in the mists of time.

I am a retired registered nurse. I enjoyed a long and happy nursing career; there were other routes I would have liked pursuing, but nursing was my true "calling." I enjoyed all lines of nursing, but home health care was my favorite and final field of practice. I found myself attending many of my patients' funerals, and this led me to writing eulogies for their wakes.

I have always written what I see and feel. I wrote many of these pieces for my church, and many others to honor my friends or family with their own poems.

I have many interests, including: genealogy, poetry, birdwatching, working puzzles and word games, collecting old books, art prints, seashells, rocks, and music of all kinds. I enjoy spending time with my family and friends. I like to sit on the porch and feed the birds.

If you enjoy this book, please let me know at:

lburgess@cmaacess.com

www.ingramcontent.com/pod-product-compliance
Lightning Source LLC
Chambersburg PA
CBHW031255110426
42743CB00039B/214